STARTING OUT

Stories for Assembly and P.S.E.

Gordon Aspland

First published 1997 by Southgate Publishers Ltd

Southgate Publishers Ltd
15 Barnfield Avenue, Exmouth, Devon EX8 2QE

Printed and bound in Great Britain by Short Run Press Ltd, Exeter, Devon.

British Library Cataloguing in Publication Data
A CIP catalogue record for this book is available from the British Library.

ISBN 1–85741–028–9

CONTENTS

Introduction

Starting Out is a collection of modern stories to be read to KS1 children. The stories look at issues and events that affect the everyday lives of young children, from looking after their belongings to issues of safety. The stories all involve the same group of six children. It is hoped that the listeners will begin to build up a picture of the characters and their personalities as the stories are told. The six child characters are all in the same KS1 class, and the main adults remain the same. Not all the stories are based at school, some are set at home or out and about.

This book is intended to be a resource to be dipped into when required. Teachers may find the stories useful for collective worship, or for classwork, particularly for P.S.E. and English. Some of the stories reflect moral values described in the N.C.C. document on *Spiritual and Moral Development* (1993), such as respecting the rights and property of others; helping those less fortunate and weaker than ourselves; acting considerately towards each other; taking personal responsibility for one's actions.

SUGGESTIONS FOR USE

In Collective Worship

This book can be picked up and the stories used just as they are by the teacher in a hurry. They take between five and fifteen minutes to read and, with a short follow-up discussion, song or hymn and prayer, or time for silent reflection, they would occupy a full assembly for collective worship of between fifteen and twenty minutes in length. More satisfactory than this *ad hoc* use is the planning of stories from the book to fit into a full-term's or year's pattern of collective worship, alongside religious material from Christianity and other world faiths. This would provide a coherent framework in which to set these 'broadly Christian' but essentially secular stories which would meet the requirements of the *Education Reform Act* that, taking a term as a whole, the collective worship must be wholly or mainly of a broadly Christian nature. Teachers may like to consult DFE circular 1/94 *Religious Education and Collective Worship* for further information on the requirements.

After each story there are questions for discussion. There is also a prayer for schools who wish to incorporate it into their act of worship. Prayer can be introduced in an open-ended way by phrases such as 'We're going to have a few quiet moments to think about ... ' or 'If you wish, share this prayer I'm going to read ... '.

In Classwork

Within the National Curriculum framework the stories might be used particularly in oral work in P.S.E. and English.

This book is not intended to be a course for P.S.E. but a resource to be used as appropriate. Certain stories are suitable for use within a structured programme of P.S.E. For example, for tackling issues of personal safety, stories such as *The Open Gate* (road safety), *Nasima's Medicine* (drugs) and *Messing About* (being silly and causing accidents) would be very useful. Some stories have a seasonal slant, such as *The Fireworks* and *Who Gave the Most* (harvest). Other stories look at simple events that pose real issues for young children, such as *The Green Coat* (a lost coat) and *What's Wrong with Thomas* (a mother who didn't say goodbye). Serious issues that affect children and parents are also included, such as in *Brandy's Gone* (bereavement of a pet), *Beware of Strangers*, and *The Little Duckling* (the environment).

By using the discussion questions after each story and oral work such as talking in pairs, children can begin to develop skills appropriate to P.S.E., such as predicting outcomes from different types of behaviours; empathizing with other people's feeling; reflecting on their own behaviour and feelings; and respecting the views and feelings of others. Skills appropriate to English can also be developed through paired work, discussion and drama. Children can be asked to make simple responses to the stories through pictures, role play/drama and writing.

Gordon Aspland
1997

STARTING OUT

1 The Green Coat

THEME: first days at school; looking after your property

Amanda held her mother's hand very tightly. She had been looking forward all holiday to going to school but now that she was walking up to the door she was very frightened. It was all so different from being at play-group, the bigger children, the huge building – what if she got lost? – and the noise of all the children playing. Well, if she had to go into the school then she was going to make sure her mother stayed with her!

"Hello Amanda, how nice to see you,' said Mrs Hughes, her new teacher. Her teacher's warm greeting made Amanda feel much better but she still clung to her mother's hand. Mrs Hughes showed her where to hang her coat. There was a metal peg with her name printed above it.

They went into the classroom and Mrs Hughes took her to a table where three other children were already sitting . Amanda recognised them from her play-group. Ranjit, Aaron and Emma all smiled at her as she sat down at the table. She let go of her mother's hand and joined the others who were playing with little coloured plastic bears. She was vaguely aware of her mother saying good-bye as she began to enjoy playing with her friends.

The morning went quickly with lots of nice things to do and just before play-time they had a story. Mrs Hughes then told them they could go outside to play. Amanda went to get her coat and it was gone!

Amanda didn't know what to do. She remembered her mother putting her coat on her peg but it wasn't there now. She had lost her coat on the first day of school! Where was it? Had somebody taken it? Amanda stood there staring at her empty peg. She became very upset. Then she started to cry.

Ranjit and Emma came up to her. "Why are you crying?" asked Emma kindly.

"My coat's not there," cried Amanda.

"I'll go and tell Miss," volunteered Ranjit.

Mrs Hughes came into the cloakroom. "Amanda, Ranjit says you have lost your coat, is that right?" Amanda shook her head. "Well it's certainly not on your peg.

What colour was it?"

"Green," choked Amanda in between sobs of crying.

"Well, there's a green coat here on Aaron's peg, is this yours?" she asked. Amanda looked at it. It looked like her coat. "I don't know," she said.

"There's no name on it so we can't tell for sure," said Mrs Hughes. She then looked out of the window and saw Aaron running around wearing a blue anorak. "I think this must be yours, Aaron has got his on. Somebody must have knocked yours onto the floor and put it back onto the wrong peg."

Amanda had now stopped crying. She put the green coat on and she immediately realised that it was her coat, it felt just right.

"I think you should ask your mum to put your name in it. Now off you go out to play," said Mrs Hughes. The three children happily went out to play.

Discussion:

1. How did Amanda's coat end up on Aaron's peg?
2. How did Emma and Ranjit help her?
3. What does Amanda's mother need to do?
4. If the coat goes missing again what should Amanda do?
5. How did Amanda feel on her first day at school? How did you feel on your first day?

Prayer:

Lord, help us to always be kind and helpful to others. If our friends lose something then we can help them to find it. Help us to look after our own things.

2
The Guinea Pig

THEME: looking after animals

The children sat around the table waiting to see what was going to happen. Mrs Hughes carefully placed a cardboard box onto the middle of the table. There was a sound of scuffling inside the box. Mrs Hughes had said she had a surprise for the children. They were now going to find out what it was!

She carefully opened the top of the box and reached inside. The children leaned closer to have a better look. She brought out a little bundle of black and white fur that wriggled in her hands. There was a big 'ahhh' from the children.

"This is Benny. Does anybody know what kind of animal he is?" asked Mrs Hughes.

"Hamster," Aaron called out.

"No, hamsters are smaller than this, will anybody else have a guess?" Emma put her hand up. "Do you know what he is, Emma?"

"No, but he's done a puddle on the table," she said. All the children laughed.

"Well, I'll have to tell you. Benny is a guinea pig. He's a bit like a rabbit but without floppy ears and a fluffy tail." There was a squeal from inside the box and Benny squealed back. Mrs Hughes reached in again and brought out another guinea pig. "This is Fluffy, Benny's mate." She put Fluffy down beside Benny and the two guinea pigs huddled together staring at the children.

"Do you know what guinea pigs eat?" asked Mrs Hughes.

"Cat food?" suggested Nasima.

"No, they are vegetarians, they only eat grass and vegetables like carrots and lettuce. They love dandelion leaves as well," explained Mrs Hughes.

"What are we going to do with them? " asked Aaron.

"You know we have been doing some writing and pictures about your pets at home? Well these are going to be our class pets for a few weeks. You can take it in turns to look after them."

The children were very excited about this and all volunteered to be first. Mrs

Hughes made a list of children to look after the guinea pigs. They had to find fresh grass and dandelion leaves from the school field. They also had to give them pieces of carrot and lettuce and check that they had enough water. Mrs Hughes told the children they could stroke the guinea pigs but not to pick them up because they could be quite lively and try to get away.

One day Aaron sneaked back into the classroom during playtime. He loved the guinea pigs . He didn't have a pet at home and he wished he could take Fluffy or Benny home with him. As he approached the cage Fluffy came out to greet him. She was always hungry and thought it was time to eat. Aaron stroked her warm, soft little body. He forgot what Mrs Hughes said and gently picked Fluffy up and cradled her in his arms.

Benny must have sensed Fluffy had gone as he came out from under the straw and made a frantic squealing noise. Fluffy heard him and called back. She began to scrabble out of Aaron's arms. Fluffy was a strong creature and Aaron couldn't hold her. She fell from his arms and dashed away amongst the chairs and tables. Aaron heard footsteps, it was the other children coming back. He hid behind the bookcase and when a few children came in and sat down he also went to his chair. Nobody had noticed him.

The guinea pigs spent a lot of time hiding in the straw so when some of the children looked into the cage they weren't surprised only to see Benny. They thought

Fluffy was under the straw. It wasn't until the end of the day when Emma was changing the water that they found that Fluffy was missing. The children were very upset. Aaron began to cry.

"Does anybody know how Fluffy got out?" asked Mrs Hughes. "She couldn't climb out on our own." She looked at Aaron who was the most upset.

"I didn't mean to," cried Aaron.

"Is she in the classroom somewhere?" appealed Mrs Hughes. Aaron nodded his head. Mrs Hughes had an idea. Whenever it was feeding time the guinea pigs would squeal with delight. She told everyone in the class to be quiet. She then went to the cage and shook the bag containing the food. Benny immediately came out squealing. Then, from the corner of the classroom, behind the play-shop, came another little squeal. It was Fluffy! She was calling for her dinner.

All the children wanted to rush over but Mrs Hughes made them sit down. She went to the corner and gently moved the play-shop. She had a lettuce leaf in her hand and she held it out for Fluffy. Fluffy was hungry and immediately began to eat. Then Mrs Hughes picked her up and carried her over to the cage. All the children were delighted, especially Aaron.

Discussion:

1. What did Mrs Hughes ask the children not to do?
2. What did Aaron do? What happened to Fluffy?
3. How did Mrs Hughes get Fluffy back?
4. How must you look after guinea pigs?
5. Why was Aaron happy at the end? Do you think he should have been punished?

Prayer

Lord, help us look after all of God's creatures. The birds in the garden, the badgers in the wood, the cats ,dogs, goldfish and guinea pigs in our homes, all need our loving care.

3
The Favourite Toy

STARTING OUT

THEME: respect for other people's property

Mrs Hughes sometimes allowed her children to bring a favourite toy to school. At the end of story time the children could show their toy and talk about it. They then put the toys on a special table. They were told not to touch them. But one day something dreadful happened, Thomas's toy went missing!

It was the day after Thomas had been on a trip to London with his parents. They had taken him to the Natural History Museum to see the dinosaurs. He just loved dinosaurs. He had pictures of them on his bedroom wall and he had little models of them on his bedside table. At night, when he was supposed to be going to sleep, he would get two or three models and play with them under his bedcover. They would have pretend fights and kill each other.

When he was at the museum his parents bought him a new model of a *Tyrannosaurus Rex*. This is what he brought to school to show the rest of the class. He proudly showed them his model, telling the other children all about his visit to the museum. On the way out to play he put the model on the special table. When he came back it was gone!

Thomas was very, very upset. He ran up to Mrs Hughes crying. "Somebody's taken my dinosaur!" sobbed Thomas.

Mrs Hughes looked at the table and the dinosaur was certainly missing. "Have you looked on the floor under the table?" she asked. Thomas shook his head. "Let's have a look, maybe it's come alive and run away. If it has we'd better be careful in case it bites our toes," she laughed, trying to cheer Thomas up.

They searched under the table but there was no dinosaur. They then began to search around the room but they still couldn't find it. The rest of the class had now come in from playtime and Mrs Hughes asked them if anybody had seen Thomas's dinosaur. Thomas began to cry again. He really was very upset.

Emma came up to Mrs Hughes and said, "I think I saw Aaron playing with a dinosaur outside."

Mrs Hughes looked at Aaron, "Were you playing with a dinosaur?" she asked. Aaron smiled happily and nodded his head. "Where is it?"

"In my bag," he replied.

"I'd like to see it, Aaron. Go and get your bag and bring it here." Aaron went to his bag and came back with a model dinosaur in his hand.

"That's mine!" shouted Thomas.

"Aaron, did you bring that from home?" asked Mrs Hughes.

"No, I found it," he said.

"Where did you find it?" carried on Mrs Hughes.

"On that table," he replied. He pointed to the special toy table.

"Why did you take it?" asked Mrs Hughes. Aaron just shrugged his shoulders, he didn't really know why. He liked the look of the model and took it. "But Aaron, this doesn't belong to you." Aaron was beginning to realise that he had done something wrong though he wasn't quite too sure what. "Do *you* have anything on the table?" Mrs Hughes asked.

"My car," said Aaron rather softly, he was getting worried now.

"Get your car and bring it to me," she said. Aaron brought the car over. "It's a lovely car, is it your favourite?" Aaron nodded. "Would you like me to give it to Ranjit to play with and keep?"

"No," he replied and his eyes began to well up with tears.

"Well," continued Mrs Hughes, "this dinosaur belongs to Thomas just like your car belongs to you. You have made Thomas very sad by taking his dinosaur, just like you would be if someone took your car. Now go and put the dinosaur back on the table and promise me you will not touch things that belong to other people."

Aaron put the dinosaur and his car back onto the table. He had learned a very important lesson about things that belong to other people.

Discussion:

1. How do we know that dinosaurs are Thomas's favourite toys?
2. What happened to the dinosaur?
3. Why did Aaron take it?
4. What did Aaron bring to show the class?
5. What lesson did Aaron learn?
6. Why do you think Mrs Hughes said that the children were not to touch things on the table?

Prayer:

Lord, help us to remember that taking something that belongs to someone else is wrong. Help us to respect things which belong to others, just as we want others to respect things which belong to us.

STARTING OUT

4 Nasima's Medicine

THEME: medicines can be dangerous

Can you imagine what would make several children in Mrs Hughes's class fall asleep? Here is what happened one day when Mrs Hughes was reading to her class. She thought it was a very exciting story, then she noticed that some of the children were literally falling asleep!

On Thursday Nasima was in the play corner. It was set up as a hospital and Nasima was pretending to be a nurse. She was giving some dollies and teddies their medicine and telling them to get better quickly. She loved pretending to be a nurse. In fact, she had already decided that when she was grown up she would like to be a nurse.

That evening her grandma, who was staying with them for a while, had gone to bed early. Nasima's mother told everyone to be quiet because their grandma had a nasty cold and cough and had gone to bed to have a rest. Nasima noticed her grandma's cough medicine by the sink in the kitchen. She remembered that quite a few children in the class had coughs so she decided that maybe she could be a real nurse and give them some medicine. Nasima took the medicine and put it in her school bag. She also found a special spoon and put that in her bag as well. She couldn't wait until tomorrow!

Nasima was very excited when she went to school the next day. It wasn't until playtime that she could be a nurse and give out her medicine. Quite a few children had coughs and she had them lined up to give them their medicine. Aaron was first in the queue and when he said 'yummy' after having a spoonful the others were quite keen to have theirs. Emma was the only one with a cough not to have any. Even though she had a cough she didn't like taking medicine. Very soon all of the medicine was gone. Some of the children had two spoonfuls, and Aaron, because he was usually greedy, had three!

Later that morning Mrs Hughes gathered the children around her for a story. Several of the children were yawning. She thought how tired they looked, maybe it was because it was the end of the week. Mrs Hughes began to read when

COUGH SYRUP
CLOTHES BOX

suddenly Aaron slumped forward, fast asleep. Mrs Hughes stopped reading and quickly went over to him and helped him to sit up again. While she was doing that, Ranjit and then Amanda nodded off as well! Oh dear, thought Mrs Hughes, something wasn't right here. She sent Mary and Ben to get Mr Hall, the head-teacher. Other children began to cry because they didn't feel well.

When Mr Hall arrived he couldn't believe what he was seeing. Something had obviously affected the children, but what? He asked those who were alright if they knew what was wrong and it was Emma who told him. She noticed that only the children who had Nasima's medicine were unwell. Mr Hall told Nasima to bring the empty bottle to him. Nasima had now realised that she had done something very wrong and she was very worried.

Mr Hall looked at the bottle and was relieved to see that it was a cough medicine that could be given to children, but only one spoonful! It also said on the bottle that the medicine might cause 'drowsiness'. If some of the children had taken more than one spoonful then no wonder they were asleep. Mr Hall telephoned the local doctor. He said that as long as no-one had taken more than three spoonfuls then they would be alright. They just needed to go home and have a good sleep.

Mr Hall then telephoned all the parents. They came and collected their children. They were not very pleased about what had happened. But the parents who were most angry were Nasima's. She was in real trouble. She should never have touched her grandma's medicine. To give someone's medicine to other people was very dangerous, as the other children could have become very ill. Her mother told her that being a nurse was all about making people better, not worse!

Discussion:

1. Why did Nasima take the medicine to school?
2. How did Mrs Hughes know that something was wrong?
3. Nasima wasn't the only one who was very silly, who else should have known better?
4. What does 'drowsiness' mean?
5. What do medicines do? What effects do they have?
6. Why can medicines be dangerous sometimes?

Prayer:

We give thanks for the doctors and nurses who look after us. They help to make us feel better when we are ill. We pray that all people who are ill will soon get well.

5 The Open Gate

THEME: road safety; school rules

Ford Street Primary School was right beside a very busy road. There were shops on the other side of the road. Cars and lorries were always stopping, turning or zooming by. A high fence surrounded the school and there was a gate leading from the road into the school grounds. There was a sign by the gate reminding parents to close the gate when they came through. The children were not allowed to go near the gate during playtimes.

When winter came the children were no longer allowed to play on the grass field behind the school. Instead they had to use the netball courts at the front of the school, next to the busy road. The one problem with this was that they had to be very careful with kicking or throwing balls in case they went over the fence onto the road. If that happened the children had to tell an adult who would then go and get the ball. But there is always one child who thinks he knows best.

It was the afternoon break when the older children were not outside. The Infants had the whole playground to themselves. It was great to be able to run around and chase after your friends without getting knocked over by the bigger ones. This was the time when the boys in Mrs Hughes' class could have a proper game of football. Today though they didn't have a proper football. A small group of children were playing football with Ranjit's old tennis ball.

Their little game was going well, Aaron and Thomas against Ranjit and Amanda. It was getting near the end of playtime and Aaron and Thomas were losing 2 – 1. The ball came to Thomas who kicked wildly at it. His heart sank when he saw it curve high over the fence onto the road. All four children stood by the fence watching the ball come to rest in the gutter on the other side of the road.

"Why did you do that?" asked an angry Ranjit. He was worried that he had now lost his only ball.

"I didn't mean it," said Thomas. "I was trying to kick it to Aaron."

"What should we do now?" asked Amanda.

FORD STREET
PRIMARY SCHOOL
PLEASE
SHUT THE
GATE
SCHOOL

"Maybe Mrs Jones will get it for us," said Aaron.

Mrs Jones was the teacher on duty. Thomas, who was feeling guilty about kicking the ball over the fence, looked for her. He saw her busy with Nasima who had fallen over. He was desperate to get the ball back. He looked at the gate and it was open! There was the ball, sitting in the gutter just on the other side of the road. There was the gate, open, inviting him out.

Thomas ran to the gate, he was through in a second. He quickly looked to see if there were any cars coming. The road was clear and he started to run across. He was in the middle of the road when a car pulled out from the parking space by a shop. It began to accelerate down the road towards Thomas. There was a loud shout of warning. Thomas stopped and stared at the car coming towards him. He was too frightened to move. The driver saw Thomas just in time and he slammed on his brakes. His car came to a screeching stop just centimetres from Thomas. A strong arm picked him up and carried him to the side of the road.

"Are you alright?" asked the man who picked him up. All Thomas could do was nod his head. He looked across the road and saw Mrs Jones coming across looking very worried.

"Thank you very much," she said to the man. "Are you alright, Thomas?" Again Thomas just nodded, he was too shaken to speak. "Why did you come out here, you know you are not supposed to go out of the gate?" With that, Thomas began to cry. Mrs Jones took his hand and took him carefully across the road towards the school gate.

"Hang on," shouted the man who helped Thomas. He walked across the road and approached them. "I think this is what the young man was after." He gave Mrs Jones the old, tatty tennis ball.

"What do you say, Thomas?" Mrs Jones asked.

"Thank you," he said.

When they entered the school grounds Mrs Jones closed the gate. She then shooed all the children away from the fence. They had all been watching what was happening to Thomas. That made Thomas feel even worse!

Discussion:

1. What school rule did Thomas break?
2. Why do you think the gate was left open in the first place?
3. What are the children supposed to do when the ball goes over the fence?
4. Why did the school have a rule about not going out of the gate?
5. What is the 'Green Cross Code'?

Prayer:

Let us quietly think about school rules and why we have them. Let us thank God for school rules. They are there for our protection, to keep us safe.

6 Messing About

THEME: behaving badly

Amanda looked at her painting, one more dab of red and it was finished. She then put her brush down and called Mrs Hughes. "Oh Amanda, what a lovely painting," she said, admiring Amanda's painting of animals in a zoo.

"That's an elephant and that's a tiger," Amanda explained.

"They look really good. I think you should tidy up now, it's getting close to lunch time," said Mrs Hughes. "You need to give your hands a good wash. I think you have just as much paint on you as you have on your painting."

Amanda took off her painting apron and walked to the toilets to wash her hands. Some of the other children were already there rinsing their hands under the taps. Ranjit and Aaron were at the same tap but Aaron was washing his hands first. Ranjit decided he had waited long enough and pushed Aaron out of the way so that he could wash his hands. This annoyed Aaron so he pushed Ranjit back. Then he filled his hands with water and threw it all over Ranjit. The boys then began to laugh and started flinging water at everybody. Amanda pulled some paper towels out, soaked them with water and flung them at the two boys. They thought that was a great idea and started to do the same. Soon the children were throwing wet paper towels everywhere; until a booming voice stopped them dead.

"What is going on here?!" shouted Mrs Hughes. "Look at this dreadful mess, can't you do a simple thing like wash your hands without being stupid? Out of here and go and sit down on the carpet."

The children very sheepishly walked out of the toilets and back to the class-room. Thomas, who hadn't been one of the naughty ones went up to Mrs Hughes. "Please miss, can I wash my hands?" He was the last one to finish his painting and needed to wash the paint from his hands.

"Alright, but be careful, there are wet paper towels everywhere."

Thomas carefully walked up to a sink and washed the paint from his hands. He turned to get a paper towel from the dispenser and stepped on a wet paper towel.

His foot shot out from under him and he fell head first towards the paper towel bin. His forehead hit the edge of the bin and he felt a sudden pain across his head. He fell onto the floor and gave a loud shriek as he felt blood dripping down his face. Mrs Hughes came rushing in, took one look at him and called for Mrs Marks the classroom assistant. Mrs Marks grabbed the first aid box and put on some special gloves. She took out a large pad and pressed it against Thomas's head.

Thomas quietly sobbed as Mrs Hughes tried to wipe the blood from his head so that she could see how badly hurt he was.

"He's got a nasty cut over his eyebrow," she said to Mrs Marks, "I think he will need to go to the hospital for some stitches. We need to telephone his parents right away."

Mrs Marks went to the office and managed to contact Thomas's mother who came to the school right away. She didn't have a car so Mrs Marks offered to drive them to the local casualty department. When they arrived at the hospital the doctor examined Thomas and was quite happy that his only damage was a cut on his head. The doctor needed to put seven stitches in it. Thomas didn't really like that but it was over very quickly. He was then allowed to go home.

Mrs Marks dropped them off at home and then went back to school. It was near the end of the school day and the class had been very quiet all that afternoon. They knew that if it hadn't been for those silly children throwing wet paper towels then Thomas would not have slipped.

Mrs Hughes was reading a story when Mrs Marks arrived back. Mrs Hughes stopped reading and asked Mrs Marks how Thomas was. Mrs Marks told her and the class all about Thomas needing seven stitches in his head.

Mrs Hughes looked towards the group of children who were the naughty ones, especially Aaron, Ranjit and Amanda. "Well I hope you realise what you have done. Who is going to tell me how you should behave when you go to wash your hands?"

Discussion:

1. How should the children answer Mrs Hughes's question?
2. What did the children do that was very dangerous?
3. What is it that can make a floor slippery?
4. Should the children be punished? If so, what should their punishment be?
5. Discuss other times when behaving badly can hurt other people.
6. Discuss the reasons why we need to wash our hands.

Prayer:

Let us quietly think about the story of Thomas, how he was hurt by other children's silly behaviour. Lord, when we are tempted to be silly help us first to think about others. Help us to remember that we may hurt others by what we do.

STARTING OUT

7

I'm Bored!

THEME: a bad attitude

Emma was in one of her moods. She felt tired and really didn't want to do any work. Whenever Mrs Hughes asked why she wasn't doing her work she just said she was bored. During maths she only completed one sum in half an hour.

"This is boring," she said to the others on her table. During writing in her diary book she put her pencil down just after two words and announced, "This is boring!"

The class's project this term was farming and in the afternoon the children were doing a mixture of activities. First Emma was in a painting group but all she did was a few squiggles of black. She then put down her brush and said it was boring. She sat down at her table and Mrs Hughes gave her group a worksheet about how we get our milk from cows. Emma got up from the table and began to wander around the room.

"Emma, why aren't you working?" asked Mrs Hughes.

"I'm bored," Emma announced.

"But the other children are enjoying the work," said Mrs Hughes, "why don't you try it?"

"I don't want to," Emma replied,"it's silly work."

"I see, well go and sit on the carpet, maybe you would like to read one of these books about farms," said Mrs Hughes.

Emma sat on the carpet and looked at a book about teddy bears. She thought books about farms were boring. After a while Mrs Hughes asked the children to put their things away and she then taught them a song about a farmer. Emma stayed on the carpet, she thought the song was boring. Mrs Hughes told the children about the assembly they were going to do for their parents. They were going to read some of their stories, sing their song and dress up as farmers. They had to bring in their dressing up clothes the next day. Emma didn't listen to any of this. She was sitting on the carpet reading her teddy bear book. Anyway, she thought farming was boring.

The next day Emma was surprised to see that the other children were carrying bags of clothes into school.

"What have you got?" she asked Nasima.

"I'm going to be a farmer in the assembly, these are my dressing up clothes," she replied. "What are you going to be?" she asked Emma.

"I don't know," said Emma. She then went over to Amanda and asked her what she was going to dress up as.

"I'm going to be a sheep," Amanda told her. Amanda brought out a sheep skin rug. She put it over her back and got down onto her hands and knees and began to baa.

Emma looked around the room. All the children were excitedly chatting to each other. Some of them came over to her and asked what she had brought in but she said she had forgotten hers. When she was asked what she was going to be she shrugged her shoulders and said she didn't know.

Mrs Hughes gathered the children together for the register. She then explained that they were going into the hall to practise for their assembly which was in two days time. There was an excited buzz when she told them about it. Even Emma felt excited until she remembered that she had nothing to wear and she didn't even know what she was going to be.

The children began to get changed for their practice. Emma sat at her desk and watched as they emptied their bags. The children put on all kinds of different clothes such as hats, coats and wellington boots. Some children had strange rugs and table cloths slung over them so they could look like farm animals. Emma sat and watched all this feeling very left out. She wanted to be in the play as well. Mrs Hughes came over to her.

"Emma, you'll have to stay in the classroom, perhaps you can help Mrs Marks tidy the library books."

"Why can't I be in the assembly?" Emma asked, nearly in tears.

"But I didn't think you wanted to be in it," explained Mrs Hughes. "Yesterday you said that everything was boring, you didn't want to take part."

Mrs Hughes sat down next to Emma. She took her hand and said softly to her, "Do you really want to be in the assembly?" Emma nodded her head and tried to smile. "Why don't you go and have a look on your peg."

Emma didn't know why she needed to look on her peg but she went anyway. When she got into the cloakroom she immediately saw that there was a plastic bag on her peg. She ran up to the bag and peeped inside. There was an old pair of her jeans, her dad's cloth cap and her wellies! Emma couldn't believe it, she was going to take part in the assembly after all. She was going to be a farmer in the play. She raced back into the classroom to get changed. The word 'boring' never entered her head again because suddenly everything was really interesting.

Discussion:

1. How do you think the bag of clothes got onto Emma's peg?
2. Why did Mrs Hughes think Emma did not want to be in the assembly?
3. Why do you think Emma changed her mind about the assembly being boring?
4. What exactly is 'boring'? Is it when you are tired, when you do not like what you are doing or when you do not know what to do? When any of these things happen what could you try to do to make it interesting?

Prayer:

Let us thank God for all the interesting things in our lives. Let us think about the different things we do in school: our writing, our number work, our music, art and PE. Let us also thank God for all the people in school who make things interesting or fun.

8
Brandy's Gone

THEME: bereavement of a pet

Amanda walked into the kitchen for breakfast. Brandy, her pet dog slowly got to her feet and wagged her tail in greeting. She hadn't been very well recently but she still managed to greet the family with a wag and a lick before flopping down again into her bed.

"Good morning, Brandy," said Amanda. She gave the dog a hug and then got her breakfast ready. Amanda's parents were already at the table eating their cereal. Usually they were talking about the day ahead but today they were very quiet. Perhaps they were in a mood with each other for some reason, thought Amanda. She just got on with her breakfast.

It wasn't until later in the day that Amanda sensed that something wasn't right. About half an hour before home time Mr Hall came into the class with a message. Amanda's mother couldn't pick her up from school so Emma's mother was going to take her home. The two mothers often helped each other out but Amanda was usually told about the arrangements in the morning. This was the first time she had been told just before home time. It was very unusual.

"Where's my mum?" Amanda asked Emma's mother.

Emma's mother looked uneasy and replied, "Oh, she's been held up, but she should be home by the time we get there." Held up where? Amanda wondered. This made her even more worried, she knew something wasn't right.

When she got home her parents were both waiting for her. Her dad wasn't at work. Her mother had obviously been crying.

"Come here, sweetheart," her mother said and held out her arms.

Amanda rushed over to her, "What's wrong, why are you crying?'

Her father put a hand on her shoulder. "It's Brandy," he said, "she's gone."

"Gone? Gone where?"

"We had to take her to the vet. He put her to sleep, a nice long sleep," he tried to explain.

"When will she come back?" Amanda continued to ask.

"She won't be coming back."

"Why?" Tears were beginning to swell in Amanda's eyes. She began to understand now.

"You know she hasn't been very well. She's very old, you know, 15 is a good age for a dog." Amanda stood there, leaning on her mother, listening. Her father continued "She hadn't been eating and she became very weak. The vet said that there was nothing he could do so he put her to sleep."

Amanda suddenly realised what they had been saying. In the past Brandy had been to the vet, even stayed there for a few days, but she always came home. This time she wasn't coming back, she had died. Amanda buried her head in her mother's lap and cried. The three of them stayed like that for some time, all very upset.

After a while they went into the kitchen to make a cup of tea. In the corner was Brandy's basket. Amanda had known Brandy all her life, Brandy had always been there. Amanda looked at the empty basket and cried again. Her father carefully lifted the basket and took it away. Nobody was very hungry that evening. Amanda went to her room early and lay down on her bed. She kept picturing Brandy in her mind, playing in the garden, running on the beach. The more she thought about her the more she quietly cried to herself. Her mother came in and tucked her into bed but she couldn't sleep.

In the morning Amanda's eyes ached. When she went into the kitchen she thought that perhaps it was all a bad dream and that she would be greeted by Brandy in the usual way. But no, Brandy wasn't there. There was just an empty space where Brandy's basket used to be. A heaviness came over Amanda and her eyes swelled with tears again.

"I don't want to go to school," said Amanda to her mother.

"You must go, love," replied her mother. "If you stay at home it will only keep

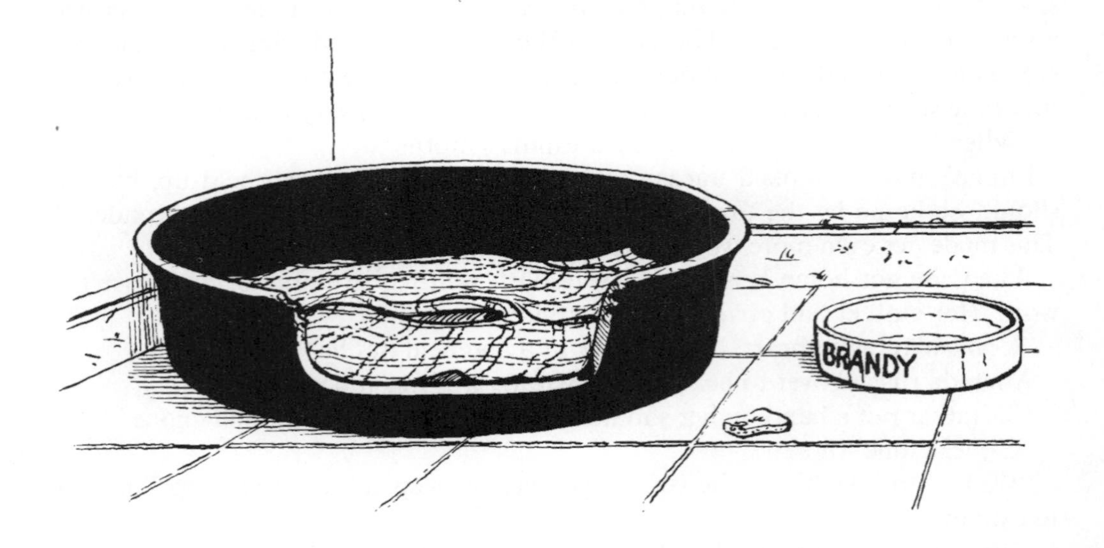

reminding you of Brandy. At school you'll be busy and you might forget what has happened."

"I won't forget Brandy!" exclaimed Amanda.

"Of course not, none of us will forget her. I meant that being at school will help you to forget how poorly she was. I'll tell your teacher so she won't fuss if you don't feel like doing too much work."

Amanda agreed to go to school. Her mother told Mrs Hughes all about Brandy. When Amanda's mother left, Mrs Hughes put her arm around Amanda and led her into the classroom.

"I know just how you must miss your dog," she told Amanda. "My dog died a few months ago and I cried because I really missed him."

That seemed to make Amanda feel a little better. Mrs Hughes understood how she felt. All day Amanda's friends were very kind to her, they shared her sorrow with her.They all knew Brandy because Amanda's mother often brought Brandy with her when she came to meet Amanda after school. Amanda didn't feel like playing or even talking but her best friends, Emma and Nasima, didn't mind. They just sat with her and kept her company.

At the end of the day Amanda felt better. She couldn't really concentrate on her work but she was glad she was with her friends. Once, near the end of the day, she told them how Brandy had become very poorly and that it was kind to put her to sleep.

When Amanda got home she quickly looked around, just in case it was all a mistake and Brandy was still there. But no, she was gone. There was no sign of her basket, her water bowl was gone and the cupboard where all her food and treats were kept was empty. It took Amanda a few weeks to get used to not having Brandy there. At dinner times she would still save a few scraps, especially the bits she didn't like, to put into Brandy's bowl. One day she got a photographic album out and asked if she could have a picture of Brandy for her bedroom wall. She would remember all the happy times she had with Brandy. Sometimes she and her parents would laugh together at the silly things Brandy used to do, such as bite the letters the postman delivered or try to catch squirrels in the garden.

Discussion:

1. When did Amanda first sense that something was wrong at home?
2. Why did her mother want her to go to school?
3. How did Mrs Hughes show she understood how Amanda felt?
4. How did her friends help her?
5. How can time help to heal the pain of losing a pet you love?

Prayer:

Lord, please watch over us when we are sad and help us to comfort others when they are unhappy.

9
The Apple Tree

THEME: fear can be a warning

It was the weekend and Thomas had invited Aaron over to play at his house. Thomas was looking forward to Aaron coming over because he had discovered a new treat in his garden. Actually, it wasn't new, it had been in the garden for as long as Thomas could remember, but he had suddenly discovered what fun it could be. He had discovered the apple tree.

The apple tree was in Thomas's garden before he was even born. In fact it was about 25 years old. It was a big, twisty tree with branches going everywhere. Thomas had not thought about the apple tree until a few weeks before when he realised he was big enough to reach the first branch. To begin with he would just sit on the first branch and pretend he was Robin Hood waiting to jump onto the rich to rob them of their gold. He loved the feel of the rough bark and the feeling of hiding in a secret spot. The leaves of the tree hid him from nosy parents who might make him get down.

Once Thomas got used to the first branch he began to explore further up the tree. With a mixture of excitement and fear, he climbed higher and higher. It took him several days before he could get close to the top. There he sat on a thin, bendy branch and he felt like the king of the castle. He couldn't wait to show Aaron his new secret hideaway.

When Aaron arrived Thomas rushed him into the garden. "I've got a great new hiding place," he excitedly told Aaron. Aaron followed him to the apple tree and watched with amazement as Thomas easily swung onto the first branch of the tree. "Come on," Thomas called, "it's great fun."

Aaron stood watching Thomas go higher. Thomas was showing off, climbing the tree quite recklessly and, a few times, he nearly slipped. He got to his top branch and called down to Aaron, "Hurry up, no-one can see us up here." That was true enough, as Aaron could hardly see Thomas through the leaves.

Aaron grabbed the first branch and swung himself up. He sat, straddled over the branch, and looked out through the leaves. Hey, this was great, he thought.

He had never climbed a tree before and this was very new to him. Thomas called again for him to hurry up. Aaron looked up for the next branch. He reached up and put his hands around the branch. He pulled himself up into a standing position. He was standing on the first branch and holding onto the next branch up. A gentle breeze waved the branches about and the sudden movement made Aaron nearly lose his balance. He grabbed onto the branch tightly, his heart was racing. He looked down and suddenly it looked as if the ground was a long way away. He had never climbed that high before and now he wished he hadn't started!

"Are you coming?" came Thomas's voice from higher up.

Aaron was gripping onto the branch, his face pressed hard against the rough bark. He didn't answer at first but when Thomas called again he shouted, "I can't!"

"You're a scaredy-cat," taunted Thomas. Aaron didn't care what Thomas called him, he just wanted to get down. It was as though the tree was alive, Aaron could feel every little movement it was making. He bit his bottom lip to stop himself from crying. After a few minutes there was a rustle of leaves above his head and Thomas popped down onto his branch.

"What's wrong, why didn't you come up?" asked Thomas.

"I don't like it up here, I want to get down," said Aaron.

Thomas could finally see that Aaron was really frightened and needed help. He tried to show Aaron how to jump down but Aaron would not let go of the branch. Thomas then ran into the house and told his mother that Aaron was stuck up the apple tree. When his mother came out she could see that Aaron was distressed. She reached up, grabbed Aaron and lifted him down. Though it was quite high for a small boy it wasn't that high for an adult.

"I think you two had better play somewhere a bit safer," she told the boys.

"Let's go up to my room and play with my LEGO," suggested Thomas. Aaron looked very relieved at this suggestion.

DISCUSSION:

1. Why was Aaron relieved to play indoors at the end?
2. Can you think why Thomas was able to get up to the top of the tree and Aaron wasn't?
3. Was Thomas fair in calling Aaron a scaredy-cat? What should he have done?
4. What things make you frightened? (E.g. the dark, spiders, heights, etc?) What could you do to help a friend who was frightened about something?
5. Fear can be a good thing, it helps us to be safe. When is fear necessary? (E.g. crossing a busy road.)

Prayer:

Dear Lord, help us to tell someone about our fears so that we shall be strong. Help us to use our fear to be safe.

STARTING OUT

10
Emma's Day

THEME: coping when things go wrong

Poor Emma, everything was going wrong for her. The day started with a rush because her parents' alarm clock did not go off. Emma was sound asleep when her mother rushed into her room to wake her up. Breakfast was a piece of bread and jam and a glass of milk before she was hurried into the car and driven to school.

"Here's some money for a school dinner," said her mother as they dashed from the car into school. "I didn't have time to make your sandwiches." Emma was a bit fussy about her food so she hoped it was something nice for lunch. She hung her coat and bag on her peg and went into the classroom.

Things continued to go wrong for Emma after assembly. Mrs Hughes asked the children to get their reading books so she could check who needed to change theirs. Emma went to her bag and was shocked to find that she only had her P.E . kit in her bag. Her reading book was not there. She took everything out but no, it definitely wasn't there. And worse, she discovered that she had also left her writing at home. She had asked Mrs Hughes if she could take her exercise book home to finish her writing. Mrs Hughes had said yes as long as she brought it back the next day. Emma had left it at home. She could picture her reading book and exercise book sitting on the chest of drawers in her bedroom at home. It was such a rush this morning, she had forgotten to put them in her bag.

Emma went back into the classroom and explained to Mrs Hughes about her reading book. Mrs Hughes wasn't very pleased and told Emma to remember her book for the next day. Emma didn't say anything about her exercise book. She was hoping that they wouldn't be doing any work on their stories that day. But her heart sank when, just before playtime, Mrs Hughes told them that when they came back in from play they were to get out their stories from yesterday.

Throughout playtime Emma worried about her writing. Eventually she became so worried that she began to cry and became very upset. When the whistle blew Amanda put her arm around Emma to comfort her. They both went into the classroom and approached Mrs Hughes.

"Why Emma, whatever is the problem?" she asked.

"She's forgotten her writing," explained Amanda.

"Oh, first your reading book and now your writing," said Mrs Hughes. She could see that Emma was upset so she talked gently to her. "You did say you would bring it back today, didn't you?"

Emma just nodded her head.

"Can you remember what you wrote?"

"Yes," replied Emma.

"Well then, there is no problem. Get a piece of paper and write down your story. Don't worry if you can't remember everything, just do what you can do," suggested Mrs Hughes.

Emma was quite happy about this. She got her pencil out of the tray and started writing on the piece of paper. Then her pencil broke. She borrowed Amanda's sharpener but the more she tried to sharpen her pencil the more it kept breaking. She could not believe this was happening to her!

"Please miss, my pencil keeps breaking," she said to Mrs Hughes in a very quiet voice.

Mrs Hughes sighed, "Oh Emma, this really isn't your day is it?" Emma smiled meekly as Mrs Hughes gave her a new pencil.

The rest of the morning went well for Emma. Then her worst fears became real when she saw what was for lunch. It was shepherds pie and cabbage followed by jelly and ice-cream. When she went up to collect her meal she asked for the smallest portion possible of shepherds pie, no cabbage and lots of jelly and ice-cream. She liked jelly and ice-cream. She was surprised that she was given what she wanted and the dinner ladies didn't say anything about her not having any cabbage. They did say that with all that jelly inside her they would have to call her Mrs Wobbly!

Emma thought that nothing could go wrong in the afternoon when they were having art and then P.E. But she was wrong. The button on the sleeve of Emma's painting shirt came off when she tried to do it up. That meant that her sleeve dangled down. Thomas put his painting brush in the jar of red paint while he went to the toilet. When Emma reached over for the blue paint, her dangling sleeve caught Thomas's brush and she knocked over the jar of red paint. It went all over her painting and Thomas's. Her day was like a bad dream. She hoped that she could close her eyes then open them again and everything would be alright. But no, the sound of Mrs Hughes's voice saying that this was the limit of her patience made her realise that it was not just a bad dream.

The ruined paintings were put in the bin and the table was cleaned up by Mrs Marks, the classroom assistant. It was near the end of art so Emma sat in the reading corner along with Thomas to wait for the others to tidy up. Thomas wasn't very pleased with her and he said so. That didn't help Emma's day.

Time for P.E., the last lesson of the day. Emma got her P.E. bag off her peg and started to get changed. She took her blouse off then her skirt. She got her t-shirt

out and put it on. She reached into her bag for her shorts and .... she couldn't believe it! She searched frantically but no, they weren't there. Emma sat down with her bag on her lap and cried. It had been a horrible day. She just wanted to go home.

The children were lining up to go into the hall, but not Emma. Mrs Hughes came over to her, and immediately she saw what was the problem.

"Emma, I just don't believe it!" But Emma stopped crying because Mrs Hughes was actually laughing! "I think maybe we should write a story about your day today. The trouble is nobody would believe it." Emma had to smile at that, it certainly had been a strange day. Amanda came over and said she had a spare leotard in her bag which Amanda could borrow.

"There now, Emma, what would you do without your friend," said Mrs Hughes. "You must remember, Emma, tomorrow is a new day and we can forget all about today."

Discussion:

1. What do you think had happened to Emma's shorts?
2. Was there anything Emma could have done to avoid having such a bad day?
3. How was Amanda a good friend to Emma?
4. What does 'tomorrow is a new day' mean?

Prayer:

Dear Lord, give us the courage to face each new day. Give us the courage to carry on when things go wrong. Show us how we can help our friends when they are unhappy.

11

The Little Duckling

STARTING OUT

THEME: looking after wildlife

The day had arrived for the class outing. The children paid one more visit to the toilet before gathering their lunch bags. Some parents were waiting with them, each clutching a list of children they were supposed to look after. They were going to spend the day at Steppes Nature Park. They had been working on a topic on mini-beasts and the ranger at the park had arranged to take them pond dipping. After lunch they were going to walk around the large lake and see how many flying insects they could find.

As the children climbed into the coach the adults laughed at the variety of hats they were wearing. It was going to be a hot, sunny day so they were all told to bring a hat. It was amazing how many different colours of baseball hats there were. There was a great debate about who was going to sit with whom, but once everyone was seated the bus started. The drive out of the city took nearly an hour but the children didn't mind. After all it was going to be a day out of school and the journey to the park was half the fun.

At the park they were met by Ranger Adams. He was a young man, tall and thin with a crop of bushy red hair. He was a jolly man who enjoyed teasing the children about their funny hats. He led the party along a path with tall trees either side. The path widened and the children became very excited as the lake came into view. It was a large lake and the children stood there trying to take in the beautiful scene. Some children thought it was the ocean though it was only several hundred metres long! But what really excited the children was all the wildlife they could see. Swans, geese, moorhens and hundreds of different ducks swam together in peace. There were 'Ohs' and 'Ahs' as a family of six ducklings with their mother swam by. Emma immediately wanted to take one home.

Reluctantly the children left the ducklings and followed Ranger Adams to another part of the lake that was shallow enough for them to stand in. They got out their wellies and carefully waded out into the water. Ranger Adams had put them into groups of four and gave each group a net with a small glass tube in the

bottom. He showed them how to carefully dip the net and then bring it out of the water. The children were fascinated by all the little creatures they could see in the glass tube. The ranger then tipped the contents of the tube into a tray so that the children could examine more carefully what he had caught. The children then had their own turn dipping their nets and looking for little creatures that lived in the water.

They worked happily like this for a while until the water became too muddy to see anything. They had a lovely morning and only three people got water in their boots. Aaron was the only one to actually fall in. He said he was pushed in by some big boys from another school. Nobody actually saw it happen but he was quite right. Aaron wanted to have a little rest so he went to the side of the lake and stood on a rock to watch the others. Three bigger boys from another school walked by. They couldn't resist giving Aaron a push and as he fell into the water they ran off into the woods. Poor Aaron, he was soaked from head to toe.

It was lunch time and the children were really hungry. Mrs Hughes had laid out most of Aaron's clothes on the grass for the sun to dry. It was a hot day and both he and his clothes dried quickly.

After lunch the children went off with their adult helpers to walk around the lake. They were looking for insects such as butterflies and dragonflies. Mrs Matthews, Emma's mother, collected Emma and her two friends, Nasima and Amanda, and they set off for their walk. But Emma was not looking for insects, she was only interested in little ducklings. As they walked along the path the three boys who pushed Aaron into the water ran past. One of them knocked Nasima's hat off and Mrs Matthews shouted at them to be careful. They had noticed other children from the same school working by the lake but these three obviously had no intention of doing what they had been told.

"There they are!" shouted Emma as she excitedly ran to the edge of the lake. The family of six ducklings were following their mother along the edge of the lake. They were soon only a couple of metres from Emma and her friends. Suddenly there was a large splash next to the ducklings.

"What was that?" said Emma.

"I don't know," replied her mother, "perhaps it was a fish jumping."

"Look over there," called Amanda, "What are those boys doing?"

Just further along the edge of the lake the three boys had collected some stones and were throwing them at the ducklings. Mrs Matthews shouted at the boys and started to run towards them when a scream from Emma brought her back. The boys had thrown another stone and it had hit one of the ducklings.

Emma was shouting "Stop it, stop it." She still had her wellies on and, without checking how deep the water was, she stepped out into the the lake. Luckily it was shallow and she managed to reach the duckling. It was lying on its side, very still. The mother and other five ducklings swam away but turned to look at Emma and quacked noisily.

Emma looked down at the tiny creature. She took off her hat and gently scooped the duckling up and carried it back to the others. "Is it alive?" she asked in a very shaky voice.

"I don't know" replied her mother, "come on, let's take it to the Ranger."

They set off quickly to the ranger's office. Ranger Adams was just about to go on his rounds around the lake when they arrived. He carefully took the duckling out of the hat and carried it into the office. He told the children to wait outside. When he came out a few minutes later he shook his head. "I'm afraid it must have been killed instantly. You say it was three boys from the other school?" Mrs Mathews explained what had happened and then a rather grim-looking Ranger Adams dashed off to find the culprits.

The three girls didn't feel like walking around the lake so Mrs Matthews took them back to the picnic area to wait for the others. As all the other groups came back, the news of the duckling spread. It was a much quieter class who climbed back into the coach. As the coach left the park they could see the ranger talking angrily with three boys and a teacher. Emma sadly thought about the duckling and how cruel the boys were. She had put her hat in her bag, somehow she didn't want to wear it again.

Discussion Points:

1. Why didn't Emma want to wear her hat again?
2. How did Aaron manage to fall into the water?
3. Why do we need to have nature parks?
4. Think of a set of rules that everyone should follow in the countryside.
5. Why do people do cruel things to helpless creatures?
6. What do you enjoy about the countryside?

Prayer:

Dear Lord, we thank you for all the creatures in our nature parks, the colourful butterflies, the shimmering dragonflies and the graceful swans. Help us to look after our countryside so that we can all enjoy it. Teach us to care for all your creatures.

12

Beware of Strangers

STARTING OUT

THEME: saying 'no' to strangers

Ranjit's mother always picked him up from school. She would be there waiting for him when he left the classroom. But not today. Ranjit walked out with the others and looked around for his mother. Other children were being greeted by their parents ,where was his mum?

"I think you had better come with me," said Aaron's mum. She took his hand and led him back to the classroom. "Mrs. Singh hasn't arrived yet," she said to Mrs Hughes, Ranjit's teacher.

Mrs Hughes looked down at Ranjit, "I'm sure she'll be here any minute, you sit here and wait." Ranjit sat down and watched the last few children leave the room. Soon he and Mrs Hughes were the only two left in the room. Where was his mother? Then he remembered that she was taking his little sister to the dentist, perhaps she was still there. The dentist was only a block away from his house, he knew the way there. He had an idea, he would surprise his mother and go to the dentist and meet her there.

At that moment Mr Shepherd, the caretaker, came into the classroom to tell Mrs Hughes that there was a telephone call for her.

"You stay there, Ranjit, I'll be back in a minute," she said. But when she left the room Ranjit stood up and ran out of the classroom door. Nobody saw him go.

It felt rather funny walking down the road on his own. The houses seemed big, closing in all around him. He didn't realise how many people there were that he didn't know. He began to feel frightened. He knew where he was going but it didn't seem the same without his mother beside him. He turned a corner and the school was now out of sight. The road was quiet, there was nobody about. A car drove by, then it stopped. As Ranjit walked by a man got out. He stood in front of Ranjit as if he was deliberately blocking his way.

"Would you like a sweet?" he asked. Ranjit stood there not knowing what to do. He remembered a policeman came into school one day and told them about not talking to strangers. Ranjit did not take a sweet, he took a step back from the man.

750

"Come on young man, I'm not going to hurt you. I'm a friend of your mother's, she sent me here to pick you up."

Ranjit stood there looking at the man, he seemed friendly enough. But he didn't know him, he had never seen him before.

"Do you really know my mum?" he asked the man.

"Of course I do, she's late from work and she asked me to pick you up, come on, in you get." He took a step closer to Ranjit, putting out a hand to guide him into the open door of the car. But something wasn't right, Ranjit realised that the man had said his mum was late from work but she didn't work!

Ranjit looked around wildly, the man was coming towards him, he was just about to grab him. Ranjit turned around and ran away back down the road. As he ran, Ranjit began to cry with fright, he wasn't sure where he was running to. He could hear the man shout something at him and then he heard the car driving away. Ranjit stopped and looked back. The man was turning around and driving his car towards him! Ranjit began to run again, he reached the corner of the road and he saw the school playground. He ran towards the playground and he saw his mother and Mrs Hughes worriedly looking up and down the road.

"Ranjit," exclaimed Mrs Hughes, "where have you been? Your mother and I have been worried sick." Ranjit couldn't say anything at first, he just hugged his mother.

"There, there, you're alright now," she said soothingly. Just then the car with the man drove by and when he saw Mrs Hughes and Ranjit's mother he sped away very quickly. Ranjit looked up and saw the car. He blurted out what had happened. Mrs Hughes took another look at the car as it disappeared into the distance.

"Good, I've got his number," she said."You had better come in while I call the police."

Discussion:

1. Why did Ranjit leave the school on his own?
2. How did he feel walking down the road on his own?
3. How did the man try to show he was a friend?
4. What did Ranjit do when the man came towards him?
5. What do you think Ranjit is going to say to the police?
6. What did Mrs Hughes mean when she said "I've got his number"?
7. What lessons has Ranjit learned?

Prayer:
Lord, thank you for all those people who love and protect us: our parents, grandparents, teachers and friends. Help them to keep us safe and guide us when we are in danger.

STARTING OUT

13 The Birthday Gift

THEME: to give is better than to receive

Amanda couldn't wait until the weekend! She was all tingly inside thinking about it. She woke up in the middle of the night thinking about it. She couldn't concentrate on her work at school because she was thinking about it. She was driving her mother mad at home because she constantly was talking about it. It was her birthday on Saturday and she was having a party!

Amanda had invited all of her friends from school and she had told them all that she was getting a Barbie doll as a present from her parents and that she would like to have lots of different clothes and other accessories. Barbie dolls were all the rage with the girls at the moment and it was only she and Emma who had not started collecting them yet.

As the end of the week came Amanda became increasingly impatient for Saturday to come. Why was it that the time seemed to go slower when she wanted it to go faster! Saturday morning finally came and she was out of bed at five-thirty in the morning. She dashed into the lounge and there was a large wrapped box with her name on it sitting on the settee. There were also three other parcels, but she tackled the big box first, it was obviously her present from her mum and dad. Wrapping paper flew everywhere as she tore the parcel open.

When she opened the box she gasped with delight as she picked out a Barbie doll, a case which held her Magic House and packs of different types of clothes. There were so many that she could have a fashion show! She then opened the other presents. The first from her Grandma contained Sprint, Barbie's pet horse. The next parcel was from her Auntie and Uncle and it was the Barbie Baywatch Rescue Station. The third parcel was from her Auntie Jean and when she opened it she was pleased to find another Barbie doll. This one could be Barbie's sister, thought Amanda.

Amanda spent the morning playing with her dolls and then she got ready for her party. Eight of her friends were coming for lunch and they were due to arrive any moment. It was then the telephone rang. Her mother answered it, spoke for a few minutes and then came into the lounge to speak to Amanda.

"That was Emma's mother, I'm afraid she isn't very well. She fell off her slide this morning and bumped her head, she's feeling sick now and they've called the doctor out," explained Amanda's mother. Amanda was very disappointed because Emma was her best friend and was going to stay the night after the party. She thought that as she now had two Barbies they could each play with one. But she soon forgot about Emma once the doorbell rang and her first guest arrived.

She had a lovely party lunch, except when Aaron spilled orange juice all over the table and Nasima cried when Thomas hit her over the head with the Barbie beach buggy he gave Amanda. When everyone had gone Amanda surveyed all the Barbie toys she was given. She felt sad because Emma wouldn't be around to play with her.

That evening Amanda's mother had worse news for her, Emma had had to go into hospital because the doctor thought she might have concussion. They had to x-ray her head to make sure she would be alright and she was going to be there for a few days.

"Can we go to the hospital to visit Emma?" asked Amanda when her mother was tucking her up in bed.

"I'm sure that would be alright, I'll telephone her mum in the morning to find out the times for visiting," said her mother. "We can pop into the newsagent tomorrow morning and buy her a little treat to cheer her up."

"Can I choose?" asked Amanda.

"Of course you can," said her mother pretending not to see the Barbie doll hiding under Amanda's bed cover. "Now off to sleep, you've had a very busy day today and you were up very early this morning. Your father is sound asleep on the settee already!" She tucked Amanda in and turned off her light. When she left Amanda quietly got her Barbie doll out but she soon fell asleep with the doll cradled in her arms.

The next day they arranged to visit Emma at three o'clock. "Are you ready to go down to the shop, Amanda," asked her mum calling from the kitchen, "they'll be closed soon so we must hurry."

Amanda walked into the kitchen holding the two Barbie dolls. "Mum, do you think Auntie Jean will be upset if I give her Barbie doll to Emma? She hasn't got one and I suppose I don't really need two."

"She gave it to you to do with as you please. I think she might be quite proud to think you gave it to a sick friend," replied her mother.

So Amanda took both of her dolls into hospital and the look on Emma's face when she gave Emma one of the dolls was something Amanda was not going to forget. The two girls played with the dolls for an hour before the nurse said that visiting time was over. Emma's mother came up to them as they were walking out of the ward and said, "Thank you very much for visiting Emma, she was feeling very low this morning but you have really cheered her up and she can't stop talking about the Barbie doll. She should be out tomorrow so I hope Amanda will be able to come over and see her."

When Amanda and her mother were walking out of the hospital Amanda turned to her mother and said, "Mum, Mr Hall said in assembly that it was better to give than to receive. I think I know what he means now. I feel really good inside."

"Even better than you felt yesterday when all your friends were giving you presents?"

Amanda thought for a minute, "That was nice but this is even better."

Discussion:

1. How did Amanda feel the day before her birthday?
2. Why did Amanda want a Barbie doll?
3. What other times do we give presents to each other?
4. How did Amanda show she cared about Emma?
5. How did Amanda's gift make Emma feel? How did it make Amanda feel?
6. What should we always say when we receive a gift? Why?

Prayer:

We all enjoy giving and receiving gifts. We pray that we always remember to say thank you when we receive a gift. Help us to remember that there are many people who do not have as much as we have.

14
What's Wrong with Thomas?

STARTING OUT

THEME: talking helps

The children sat quietly listening to Mr Hall, the head teacher. It was assembly time and Mr Hall was reading a story to the school. Then, in the middle of the story, crying could be heard. Mr Hall stopped and looked down. At first he couldn't see where the crying was coming from, but then he noticed Thomas with tears streaming down his red face.

"Come here, Thomas," Mr Hall said gently. Thomas stood up, stepped around the children sitting in front of him and walked up to Mr Hall. Mr Hall bent down and quietly said, "Thomas, whatever is the matter?"

Thomas didn't answer, he just cried a little louder. There were murmerings from some of the other children in the hall, one girl giggled cruelly. Mr Hall glared down at that rude girl and then took Thomas by the hand and led him out of the hall to find Mrs Hughes, Thomas's teacher.

"There you are Mrs Hughes, I'm afraid Thomas is rather upset about something." Mr Hall handed Thomas over to Mrs Hughes and then went back into the hall to finish his assembly.

Mrs Hughes put a reassuring hand on Thomas's shoulder and said,"This is most unlike you, Thomas, what's the matter?"

But Thomas did not answer, he continued to cry, rubbing his eyes with his fists.

"Are you feeling alright?" Again, Thomas did not answer.

"Do you have a headache or a tummyache?" Mrs Hughes asked. There was still no answer.

"Thomas, please tell me what is the matter. Has somebody been nasty to you?"

There was still no answer.

"Has something happened at home?"

There was still no answer.

"Come on, Thomas, I really can't help you if you don't tell me what is wrong."

Thomas continued to be very upset. It was obvious he wasn't going to say what was wrong with him.

Mrs Hughes took him into the office where Mrs Roberts, the school secretary, was busy with the dinner registers. She looked up from her work and said, "Oh dear, is Thomas not well?"

"I don't know what is wrong with him," replied Mrs Hughes. "I think I'd better telephone his mother and see if she knows."

Mrs Hughes picked up the telephone and dialled Thomas's number. After a few seconds she began to talk to Mrs Allen. When she put the telephone down Mrs Hughes said, "I'm afraid Mrs Allen doesn't know what the problem is either. She's coming up to the school right away."

Mrs Hughes sat Thomas down on a chair outside the office. Her class was still in assembly so she was able to wait with until Thomas's mother arrived. They only had to wait a few minutes when Mrs Allen came through the school doors.

"Thomas, what's the matter?" she asked as he ran over to her. Thomas stopped crying and whispered something into her ear. She then gave him a hug and a kiss and said, "I'm sorry, love, I was in such a hurry to get back home because Auntie Margaret is coming this afternoon." Mrs Allen faced Mrs Hughes and explained, "I'm afraid Thomas is upset because I didn't say good-bye to him this morning. His auntie is coming to stay for a few days and I wanted to get home right away and tidy up. I just forgot, I'm sorry about all the fuss, I'm sure he'll be alright now."

"I'm just glad we've sorted him out," said Mrs Hughes. She looked down at Thomas and said, "if you had told us earlier why you were upset perhaps we could have helped you sooner."

Discussion:

1. What was it that upset Thomas so much?
2. Who should you tell if you are upset?
3. What should Thomas have done?
4. If you see someone is upset how can you help them?

Prayer:

Let us be thankful that we have people to talk to who will listen to us: our friends, our teachers and our parents. Help us to be brave and to tell some-one if we are unhappy.

STARTING OUT

15 It's Not Fair!

THEME: coping with teasing

Aaron Frederick Pinny was a very unhappy boy. He had been told off by Mrs Hughes for kicking George, a boy in another class. And it wasn't his fault! Well, he did kick George, but George was being horrible to him. George was *always* being horrible to him, and Aaron was the one who was *always* getting into trouble. It wasn't fair!

"Not you again," said Mrs Hughes, "you know, Aaron, you must learn to play nicely outside. It looks like you will have to miss another playtime. Come on, you can help me get the paints ready." Aaron preferred to be outside playing football.

The other children came in from the lunch break, they were excited because they were going to paint. Everyone was excited except Aaron, who just sat there with a miserable face. He eventually painted a picture but his heart wasn't in it. He was wondering if he was going to be allowed to go out to play again that afternoon. He was wondering if George was going to be out there.

Just before playtime Mrs Hughes stood beside him. "Do you think you can go out and play nicely, without kicking anybody?" she asked him. Aaron nodded yes. "Go on then, off you go." Aaron wasn't too sure if he was pleased or not. He wanted to play football, but then there was George.

The children went outside. Thomas had the class football, he threw it onto the ground and they all started chasing after it.

"Hey, Skinny Pinny, you're useless at football." Aaron stopped and turned around. There was George, shouting at him, calling him the usual names. George knew exactly how to make Aaron angry. Aaron's surname was Pinny and George called him 'Skinny Pinny'. "Skinny Pinny, Skinny Pinny, Skinny Pinny," George kept taunting him. Aaron stood there, glaring at him. He felt his body go tight, his face red and you could see sparks coming out of his eyes.

"Don't call me that," Aaron shouted through clenched teeth.

George shouted "Skinny Pinny," once more and that made Aaron lose his temper.

He ran at George and pushed him over so hard that George fell and hurt his arm, and started to cry.

"Aaron Pinny, come here!" shouted Mrs Hughes from her classroom window. Aaron walked dejectedly back to the classroom, he didn't look at George who had stopped crying and was grinning at him.

"Aaron, I saw you push George over, why did you do it?" asked Mrs Hughes when Aaron arrived in the classroom.

"He's horrible to me," he cried, bursting into tears.

"That's no excuse for hitting and kicking people," said Mrs Hughes.

"Please Miss, it really isn't Aaron's fault," said a voice from behind them. Ranjit stood by the door, he had followed Aaron into school.

"Come here, Ranjit, perhaps you can tell me what's going on," suggested Mrs Hughes.

"George is always saying horrible things, calling people names," explained

Ranjit. "He keeps calling Aaron 'Skinny Pinny'. It's not very nice."

Mrs Hughes went to the window and looked out, George was not playing with the other boys. She could see him shouting something at Thomas and she suddenly realised what had been going on. "Thank you, Ranjit. Now Aaron, just because George calls you names it doesn't mean you should hit him."

"But I don't like it!" cried Aaron.

"I know it isn't very nice, but don't you realise you are doing exactly what George wants you to do?" Aaron stopped crying and gave her a puzzled look. "George is jealous of you, you've got lots of friends and he hasn't. He is deliberately trying to get you into trouble, and he is succeeding! You've got to show him that what he is saying isn't going to bother you one little bit. Once he realises that then he'll leave you alone." Mrs Hughes told him exactly what he should do the next time George called him names. She then let him go back outside to play. As Aaron and Ranjit went out she walked over to the window to see what was going to happen.

Aaron and Ranjit rejoined the other boys in their game of football.

"Skinny Pinny, Skinny Pinny," shouted George when he saw Aaron outside again. All the boys stopped playing football to watch what was going to happen next. Aaron slowly walked up to George; his body was tense with anger.

He looked at George and said, "Don't call me names. It's stupid." He then turned around and started playing football again. George tried calling out again but Aaron just ignored him.

Mrs Hughes watched from the window. She had seen Aaron go up to George, say something and then turn away and carry on playing football with his friends. She watched George walk away, all alone. She sighed, she would have to do something about George.

Discussion:

1. How did Aaron feel inside when he was being teased?
2. Why was George teasing him?
3. How did Ranjit help Aaron?
4. What did Mrs Hughes tell Aaron to do?
5. How do you feel towards George?
6. What should Mrs Hughes say to him?
7. What is the best way to deal with teasing?

Prayer:

Let us sit quietly and think about the things we say to each other. Lord, help us to try to be kind and gentle to others. Help us not to push or hit others, however nasty they are to us.

STARTING OUT

16
Who Gave The Most?

THEME: it's not how much you give, but what it means to you

This is a story of two girls, Amanda and Emma. It was the Harvest Service and the children were asked to bring food to school. The food was going to be distributed to elderly people in the neighbourhood. Amanda brought in a huge bag of apples, enough to go to several people. Emma brought in one tin of spaghetti hoops. Who do you think gave the most? Here is how they got their gifts.

It was Friday evening and Amanda was telling her parents about what Mr Hall had said in assembly that morning. On Monday they were going to have their Harvest Service and he wanted all the children to bring in some food. "What can I take?" she asked her parents.

"How about some apples, I'll be picking them this weekend," suggested her father. "You can help me so you can say that you picked them yourself."

"Can I pick a really big bag?" Amanda asked.

"As big as you can carry," laughed her father.

The next day, after lunch Amanda's father announced he was going to pick the apples. He went outside to start picking but Amanda did not join him. She wanted to see the end of some cartoons on the television.

"Are you going to help your father?" asked her mother.

"In a minute, after this is finished," she replied. But just as she turned off the television the door bell rang. It was Nasima, her friend from school. She wanted to know if Amanda could go to her house to play. She lived across the road.

"Can I go over to Nasima's house?" she asked her mother.

"What about helping your father with the apples?" her mother reminded her.

"I'll help later when I come back," she said. Her mother let her go. Amanda came back later than she thought and her father had picked all of the apples. Amanda was upset that he had finished but it was her own fault, she had decided to do other things instead.

Emma's weekend was very different. On Saturday morning Emma asked her mother if there was anything she could take to the Harvest service.

"Oh, I don't know, love," her mother said, "we haven't got much to spare."

"Could we buy something from the shops?" asked Emma hopefully.

"If I've got any spare cash then we'll get you something," replied her mother.

Before going out to the shops Emma searched her bedside table for her special pot where she kept any pocket money she managed to save. She found two twenty pence pieces and a ten pence piece. Putting this money into her pocket she raced downstairs and followed her mother out of the door to catch the bus into town.

Emma and her mother walked up and down the supermarket aisles putting their weekend food into the trolley. When they were beside the tinned food Emma looked at the coloured labels. She spotted the tin she was after, her favourite spaghetti hoops, and put it into the trolley.

"What are you doing?" asked her mother. "Please don't put anything into the trolley without showing me first or else I'll have a right shock when I've got to pay."

"I thought this might be a good tin to take to the Harvest Festival. Look, I've got some money to pay for it," said Emma, pleading to keep the tin. She held out her money, it was in fact more than enough to pay for the tin.

Her mother smiled, "I'll tell you what, you keep the tin separate from the rest of our things and then you can pay the cashier for your tin yourself."

"Do I have enough money?" Emma wasn't quite sure how much she had and how much the tin cost. Her mother checked her cash. She looked at the price of the tin, which was 27 pence. She told Emma that she had plenty there and she would get some change.

Monday morning came and the two girls walked into school, both carrying their harvest gifts. Amanda was carrying her bag of apples and Emma her tin of spaghetti hoops. Who do you think gave the most?

Discussion:

1. Why do we bring gifts of food for our Harvest Service?
2. Why didn't Amanda help her father?
3. Did she make any effort at all to pick the apples?
4. How much effort did Emma make to get her harvest gift?
5. Amanda's gift of apples was bigger than Emma's gift of a tin of spaghetti hoops. But Emma's gift was more important, why?

Prayer:

Let us think about harvest time. Let us be thankful for our food. Let us think about what we give to others. Lord, teach us to make an effort when we give.

17

The Fireworks

THEME: taking care with fireworks

Aaron looked out of the window once again. "I think it's dark enough" he said. "Can we have the fireworks now?" It wasn't fair, he could hear fireworks going off in other gardens and it really was dark now. His father looked out of the window, checked his watch and announced it was indeed time to light the bonfire and let off the fireworks!

Aaron's older brother, Stephen, came tumbling down the stairs in his excitement and all the family trooped outside to watch. All except Bonny, their pet dog, who stayed indoors. First Aaron's father lit the bonfire and there was an 'Oooh' as the pile of wood flared up. There was soon a warm orange glow in the garden.

"Now stand well back while I light this rocket," warned Aaron's dad. He took the rocket out of the tin box and set it on its stand. He then lit a long taper, touched the end of the taper to the rocket and stood back. For a few seconds nothing happened, then the end of the rocket flared and off it went up into the sky to explode into a shower of brightly coloured sparks. More rockets with different colours followed, then catherine wheels and large bangers that seemed so loud that the windows shook. To finish with they had a string of Chinese crackers that fired away like a machine gun.

It was all over too quickly for Aaron, he wanted it to go on all night. The bonfire had now died down so his mum brought out hot-dogs to roast on the dying embers. It was a great evening and though their fireworks were finished they were able to enjoy watching other people's rockets shoot up into the night sky. Aaron took a long time to get to sleep that night because he lay in bed listening to the occasional bang in the distance.

The next morning was Sunday, and it was chilly but bright. Aaron and Stephen were up at the same time and after breakfast they went into the garden to see the dead fireworks. There was still a smell of gunpowder in the air as they pushed the exploded rocket cases over with their feet. "Hey Aaron, come over here," called Stephen. Aaron ran over to him and looked at what he was holding. "Some of

these Chinese crackers haven't exploded. Look, this one has still got a bit of a wick." The cracker was about the size of your little finger, red in colour with a little white wick sticking out of the end. Usually this was attached to all the other wicks and the crackers would go off one after the other. This one had not gone off and it still held its explosive powder.

"Wait here," said Stephen, "I'm just going to get something." He raced indoors, quickly looked around to make sure his parents were still in bed, opened a kitchen drawer and took out a box of matches. He ran outside to Aaron who was still carefully holding the cracker.

"Are you going to light it?" asked Aaron.

"Yes, it's only one little bang. Here, give it to me," said Stephen. He put the cracker onto the ground and took a match out of the box. Aaron leaned over to watch him. He lit the match and held it against the wick. It spluttered into life and both boys ran back away from it. Just as suddenly as it flared up, it died again. "It must be wet," explained Stephen. At that moment he heard his mother calling them, so, carefully putting the matches into his pocket he motioned to Aaron that they had to go in.

But Aaron was fascinated by the cracker. He walked up to it and looked down. The wick had disappeared. The cracker looked quite dead. He bent down to pick it up and just as his fingers touched the little red cylinder it exploded. It wasn't a big bang but to Aaron it seemed as if the whole ground had exploded.

The shock sent him sprawling backwards. He was vaguely aware of his brother running over to him and saying "Are you all right?" He then began to scream but it was more from fright than from pain because he couldn't feel anything with his hand. His father came running out, lifted him up and carried him into the house, while shouting for his mother to telephone an ambulance.

Aaron went to hospital but was only checked over by a doctor and then allowed home. He was lucky, it was a very small firework and, apart from his fingers being black and a little numb, he was all right. If the cracker had been closer to his face then it would have been a different story.

Discussion:

1. What could have happened if the firework had gone off closer to Aaron's face?
2. What did Stephen do that was very naughty?
3. What lesson did both boys learn? What should they have done when they found the cracker that hadn't exploded?
4. What is the 'Firework Code'?

Prayer:

We pray that everyone will enjoy fireworks and that nobody will end up in hospital. Teach us to take care with fireworks and follow the 'Firework Code'.

18

The Sting

THEME: controlling anger

When Thomas first started school he was a very naughty boy. He did something that upset many other children. It upset the other children so much that they did not want to play with him. It was a horrible thing he kept doing. It was so horrible that even the parents of the other children kept asking Mrs Hughes, the class teacher, what she was going to do about it. Do you want to know what it was? Well, when he got angry with someone he would bite them! Isn't that horrible? Would you like to be bitten by someone? Here is how it started.

One day Thomas was outside playing football with Aaron and Ranjit. He was just about to kick the ball when Ranjit kicked it away. Thomas was so angry he ran after Ranjit and bit him on the arm. Ranjit howled in pain and the other children called to Mrs Hughes and told her what had happened. She took both boys indoors. Thomas was told to sit on his own while she put a medi-wipe on Ranjit's arm. When Ranjit stopped crying he was allowed to go back outside but not Thomas, he had to stay in. Mrs Hughes was very cross with him and he wasn't allowed to go to play again that day.

A few days later he did it again. This time he was playing on the carpet with Amanda, building bridges with wooden blocks. He had built a lovely bridge when Amanda accidentally knocked it with her foot. Thomas got so angry that he leaned over and bit her on the leg! Amanda screamed so loudly that half the school heard her. This time Mrs Hughes took Thomas to see Mr Hall. He was very angry and made him stand outside his office to think about what he had done. After school Mrs Hughes told Thomas's mother about what had happened. Her face was like thunder when she took him home and he wasn't allowed to watch his favourite television programmes. But do you think Thomas learned his lesson?

The very next day he did it again. He bit poor Ranjit again. Thomas wanted to borrow Ranjit's ruler but Ranjit didn't like Thomas any more so he said 'no'. This

made Thomas cross so he bit Ranjit on the arm again. Mrs Hughes was furious. She marched him down to Mr Hall again. Mr Hall made Thomas stand outside his office again while he telephoned Thomas's mother. Ranjit's mother was also furious as this was the second time Ranjit had been bitten. Everyone was very, very angry with Thomas, but it wasn't any of these people who made him see sense. A tiny creature with a big sting finally made Thomas realise how horrible it was to bite.

Later that week Thomas was eating his packed lunch. It was that time of year when wasps are a nuisance. A wasp started to buzz around Thomas's orange drink. Thomas tried to smack it away but this made the wasp angry. It buzzed around Thomas's head, landed on his nose and gave him a dreadful sting. Thomas screeched with shock as he felt a sharp pain in his nose. Everyone in the dinner hall went quiet as the dinner ladies rushed over to him.

"Get it off, get it off!" he shouted but the wasp had already flown away. The dinner lady led him to the first aid box where she put a medi-wipe on his throbbing nose. When Thomas went back into the classroom after lunch he didn't get any sympathy from Mrs Hughes.

"I think it serves you right," she said. Thomas didn't understand why she wasn't very kind to him. "That wasp stung you because it got angry with you, just like when you bit the other children when you got angry. It wasn't very nice, was it?" Thomas nodded, he understood now what she meant. When the other children saw his red, lumpy nose they all laughed at him. He was a very unhappy boy.

Thomas learned what a nasty, horrid thing it was to bite other children and he didn't do it again. He became a very pleasant boy who eventually had lots of friends.

DISCUSSION:

1. Why wasn't Mrs Hughes very sorry for Thomas when he was stung by a wasp?
2. What lesson did Thomas learn in the end?
3. How should we behave when we get angry?
4. How should we treat our friends?

PRAYER:

Dear Lord, teach us to be kind and gentle to our friends. Help us to control our anger and to be understanding and patient. Help us to treat our friends in a way we would like them to treat us.

19
Emma's Watch

STARTING OUT

THEME: pride comes before a fall

Mrs Matthews looked out of the window again. She looked at her watch one more time. First ten minutes late, then fifteen and now 20 minutes late. This was the first time she had allowed Emma to visit her friend, Amanda, on her own. She was due back at six o'clock and it was now twenty past six. Mrs Matthews thought about telephoning but then remembered that Amanda's parents didn't have a telephone.

"Right, George," she said to Emma's little brother, "let's go and see where your sister has got to." She hastily picked George's up and opened the front door. But she didn't go out, for standing there was a very worried looking Emma. Her mother's feelings turned from relief to anger as she said, "Where have you been?"

This is what happened to Emma. Listen carefully and decide at the end if it was her fault or not.

Earlier that day Emma very proudly left her house to go to Amanda's. She had been begging her mother for weeks to let her go on her own. Her mother said she needed a watch so that she could come home at the right time. So Emma saved up her pocket money and found a lovely watch in the market. She was very proud of this watch. It had a pink face and a yellow plastic strap. Her mother then said she needed to learn how to tell the time so Emma worked really hard in order to learn. She did so well that she drove her parents mad, she was always reminding them about the time, "it's four o'clock now," "it's four-thirty now," and so it went on. Finally her mother agreed. The evenings were getting lighter and Emma had a watch to remind her about the time.

"Do you know what six o'clock looks like?" asked her mother.

"Yes, the big hand points straight to the top and the little hand points straight to the bottom," replied Emma holding her watch up. Unfortunately for Emma she did not realise that her watch was not waterproof.

When she arrived at Amanda's they immediately went to Amanda's bedroom to play with her collection of dolls. Emma showed her the watch and said that she was allowed to wear it all the time. They were enjoying playing together though Amanda was getting a little annoyed with Emma because she would keep telling her the time. Emma knew that Amanda hadn't yet learned how to tell the time. Emma was very proud of her watch and of her ability to tell the time, especially when her friends couldn't.

After a drink of juice and some biscuits the girls decided to give the dolls a bath. They took the dolls into the bathroom and began to fill up the bathtub. Amanda got a bottle of deep blue bath foam and put two capfulls in. Soon the bath was full of sweet scented bubbles. Amanda suggested that Emma take her watch off, but Emma said it was a brilliant watch and was waterproof. She checked

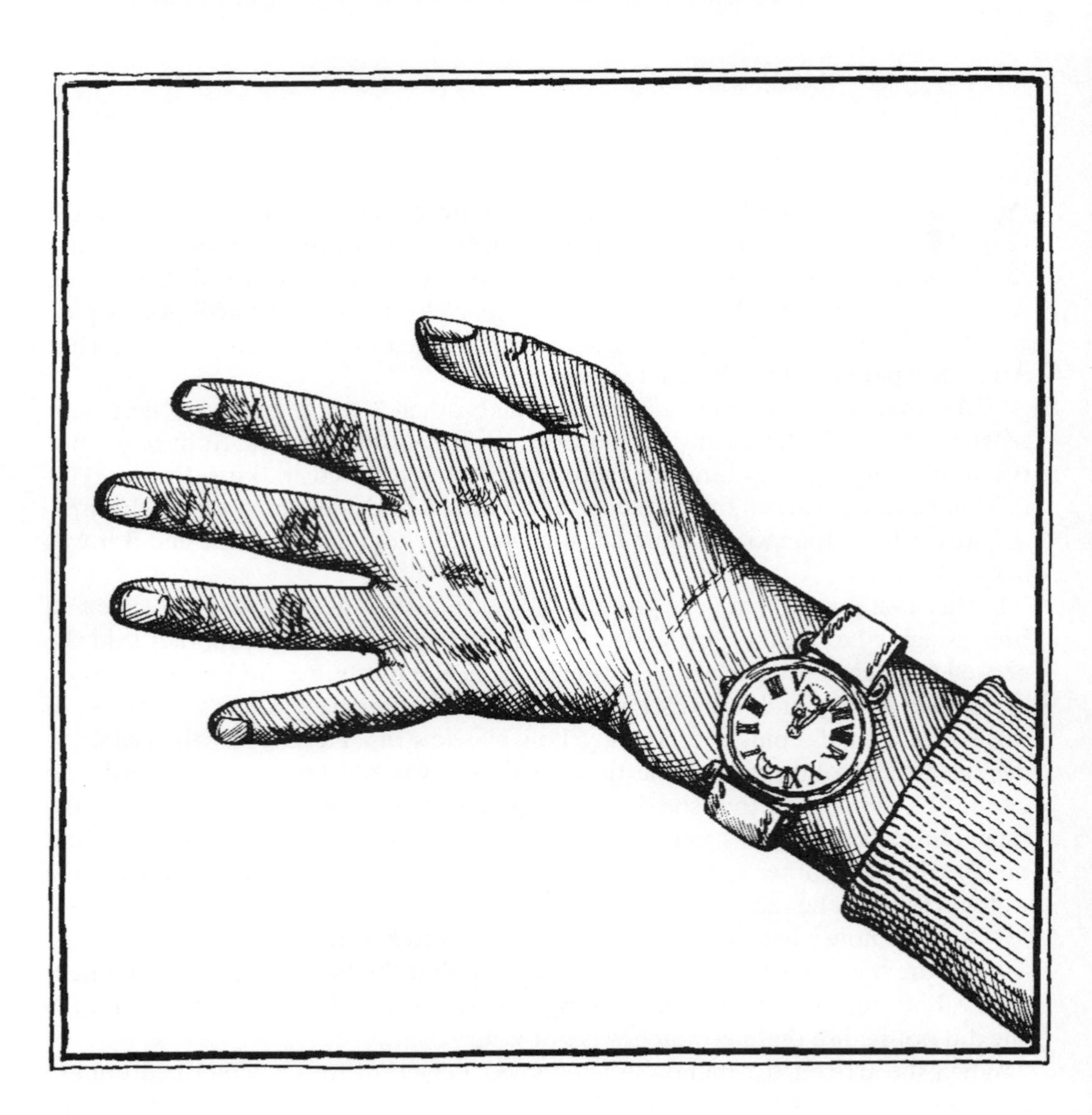

her watch and announced it was five-thirty. Then she and Amanda delved into the bubbles, squealing with delight. They threw bubbles at each other and soon they had bubbles dripping everywhere. They had so much fun that they even forgot about the dolls in the bath.

Emma brushed some bubbles off her watch and checked the time. It said five-thirty. That's strange, thought Emma, that's what it said a while ago. She decided she must have read her watch wrongly the last time and continued to play with the bubbles.

The girls stopped abruptly when a voice behind them shouted, "What are you two doing? Look at this mess!" It was Amanda's mother and she wasn't very happy. "I thought you had to go home at six o'clock, Emma."

"Yes, but it is only five-thirty," replied Emma.

"That's what you think, but it's well past six o'clock."

Emma looked at her watch. She couldn't read it properly because it was covered in wet bubbles. She rubbed the face of her watch but she still could not read it because the bubbles had got inside the watch. Her watch had stopped because of the water inside. She quickly dried her hands and was about to race downstairs when Amanda's mother said she would walk her home. When Emma got home she was in real trouble.

Discussion:

1. What did Emma have to learn to do before she could go to see her friends on her own?
2. Why was Amanda getting annoyed with Emma?
3. What do you think about Emma's behaviour?
4. Was it her fault that she was late home?
5. How do you think Emma's mother felt when Emma was late home?
6. How did Emma feel when she got home?

Prayer:

Dear God, help us always to think of others and be sensitive to their feelings. Help us not to be boastful.

20 The Little Mouse

THEME: celebrating success

The picnic was just as good as Ranjit had imagined it would be. He couldn't remember a better day. His mother had asked him what he wanted to do for a party. She couldn't believe it when he said he didn't want a party, he wanted to go into the countryside and have a picnic with his family. His two sisters thought it was a crazy idea, his father wondered when he could find the time away from the restaurant. But his mother said that if he wanted a picnic, then a picnic he'd have. And it really was a lovely day.

Ranjit got the idea for a picnic when a man from the Countryside Commission came to talk to the children in the school about how we should look after our countryside. Ranjit and most of his friends lived in the city. They never really visited the countryside. The man showed them a video showing meadows and rivers, woods and hills. He made it all sound so nice that Ranjit wanted to go out and explore the countryside. His birthday picnic was just perfect, that is until there was a loud frightened scream from one of his sisters!

They were playing hide 'n seek and Subatra was hiding behind some bushes. She came running out shouting, "There's a rat, a big horrible rat!" Ranjit's father searched through the bushes and came out holding an old lemonade bottle. Inside it was a little mouse but it wasn't moving.

"What's wrong with it?" asked Ranjit.

"I'm afraid it got into the bottle searching for food but could not get out," explained his father.

"Why couldn't it get out?"

"I suppose the sides of the bottle are too slippery."

"Why isn't it moving? Is it dead?" asked Ranjit again. He was very concerned about this poor little creature.

"Yes, it wasn't a nice way to die, was it?" said his father.

"How did the bottle get here?"

"Lots of people come here for picnics. I think somebody just threw their rubbish into the bushes," said his father. Ranjit thought about this and looked around to make sure they had picked up all their rubbish.

The next day was back to school as normal. Mrs Hughes, Ranjit's teacher, asked the children about their weekend. Ranjit told her and the rest of the class, about his picnic and the little dead mouse. Mrs Hughes said that perhaps he could write about it in his story book. Writing about what they did over the weekend was the normal routine on a Monday morning. Ranjit usually found this very difficult to do because most of his weekends were the same. In fact he didn't like writing at all, he would sit looking at his blank piece of paper wondering what to write about. He found it very difficult to find the right words to begin with.

But this time it was different. Ranjit was bursting to put his story onto paper. Mrs Hughes had never known him to come up to her to ask for so many words. He wrote about the drive to the countryside, the food they ate and the games they played. That was the first page. On the next page he wrote about finding the little mouse, only this time the mouse wasn't dead but still alive. His third page was all about taking the mouse home and getting it out of the bottle, about feeding it and keeping it warm. The final page was about taking the mouse back to the spot where it was found and letting it go. And every time Ranjit returned to the same place for a picnic the little mouse would come out and say hello.

It was a wonderful story, it took Ranjit all morning to write and then he wanted to take it home to finish. It was the best story he had ever written. The next day he showed it to Mrs Hughes. He stood proudly, quietly, by Mrs Hughes desk while she read it. When she finished she looked at Ranjit, "I don't know what to

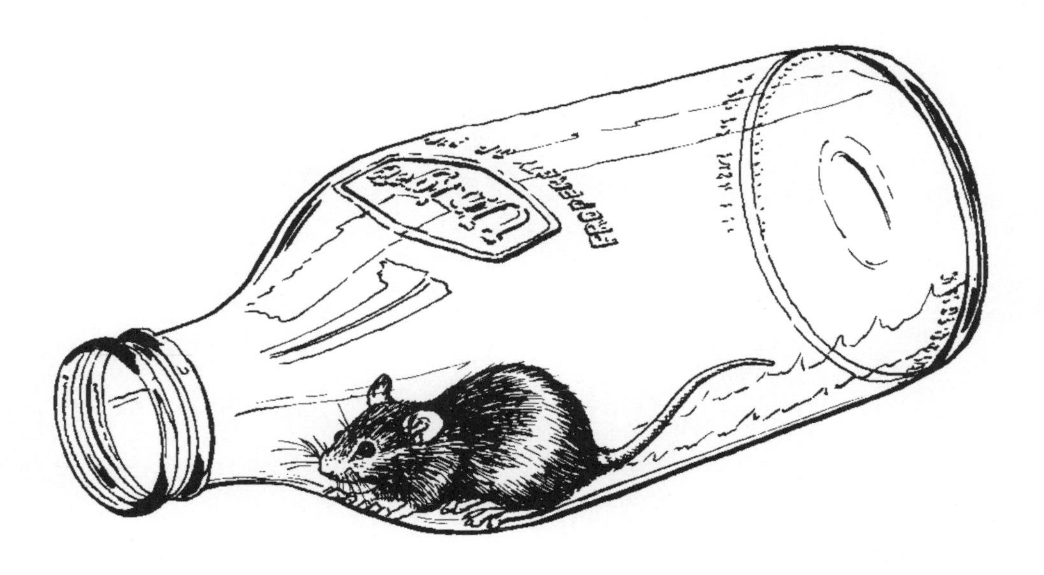

say, Ranjit, you normally don't write more than two lines for a story, but here, in front of me, is one of the best stories I have ever seen from anybody in my class. Can I read it to the rest of the class?"

When she had finished reading the story to the class they all clapped Ranjit. They also recognised that this was an extra special story. His two friends, Aaron and Thomas, both said it was a brilliant story. Later that week Ranjit was given a special merit certificate for his story by Mr Hall during the school assembly. Ranjit had never felt so good before.

Afterwards, during the weeks that followed, Ranjit's stories were not quite as long as the one about the little mouse. But that didn't worry Ranjit, he couldn't wait to start writing.

Discussion:

1. Why was Ranjit now really keen to write?
2. Describe the story Ranjit wrote.
3. What was the reaction of the other children in the class?
4. Why is it good to say well done to someone?

Prayer:

Lord, help us to notice and praise the good things other people do. During the day today let us try to say something really nice to someone. Let us praise someone for a lovely piece of work or say well done for being successful in a game.